W9-ANF-095

Watching the Seasons
Spring
by Emily C. Dawson

Bullfrog Books

Ideas for Parents and Teachers

Bullfrog Books let children practice nonfiction reading at the earliest reading levels. Repetition, familiar words, and photo labels support early readers. Here are some tips for reading with children.

Before Reading
- Discuss the cover photo. What does it tell them?

- Look at the picture glossary together. Read and discuss the words.

Read the Book
- "Walk" through the book and look at the photos. Let the child ask questions. Point out the photo labels.

- Read the book to the child, or have him or her read independently.

After Reading
- Prompt the child to think more. Ask: What is spring like where you live? What do you like to do in spring?

Bullfrog Books are published by Jump!
5357 Penn Avenue South, Minneapolis, MN 55419
www.jumplibrary.com

Library of Congress Cataloging-in-Publication Data
Dawson, Emily C.
Spring / by Emily C. Dawson.
    p. cm. -- (Watching the seasons) (Bullfrog books)
 Summary: "This photo-illustrated book for early readers describes how spring weather affects the actions of animals, the growth of plants, and the activities of people. Includes photo glossary."--
Provided by publisher.
 Includes bibliographical references and index.
 Audience: Grades K-3.
 ISBN 978-1-62031-014-4 (hbk.)
 1. Spring--Juvenile literature. I. Title.
QB637.5.D29 2013
508.2--dc23

                                    2012009112

Series Editor: Rebecca Glaser
Series Designer: Ellen Huber
Photo Researcher: Heather Dreisbach

Photo Credits
Alamy, 14–15, 18; Dreamstime, 1, 3b, 3t, 5, 6–7, 23bl, 23tl, 23tr; Getty Images, 10, 21; Shutterstock, 3b, 4, 9, 11, 12, 13, 16, 19, 20b, 20t, 22, 23br, 24; Superstock, 8, 17

Printed in the United States of America at Corporate Graphics in North Mankato, Minnesota.
7-2012 / 1124
10 9 8 7 6 5 4 3 2 1

Table of Contents

Spring is New

In spring, new things grow.

Snow melts.

Flowers poke up.

In spring, tree buds grow.
Buds grow into blossoms.
Apple blossoms are white.

bud

In spring, robins make nests.
They weave grass and twigs.

Mama robin lays eggs.

In spring,
spiderlings hatch.

They spin a
silk string.

They swing to
a new home.

silk

In spring, lambs
are born.

Mama sheep
feed them milk.

In spring, days get longer.

The sun sets later.

Cal plays outside after supper.

In spring, it is muddy.

Jen walks to school.

She wears boots.

In spring, it is windy.
Shen flies a kite.

What do you do in spring?

Watching the Seasons

Spring

Summer

Winter

Fall

Picture Glossary

blossom
A flower that grows on a fruit tree.

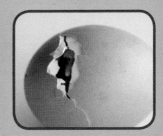

hatch
When a young animal breaks out of an egg.

bud
A small shoot on a plant that grows into a leaf or flower.

nest
A place built by birds to lay eggs and where the baby birds live after they hatch.

Index

To Learn More

Learning more is as easy as 1, 2, 3.

1) Go to www.factsurfer.com

2) Enter "spring" into the search box.

3) Click the "Surf" button to see a list of websites.

With factsurfer.com, finding more information is just a click away.